FRANK LLOYD WRIGHT FURNITURE

PORTFOLIO

Text & Photographs by
Thomas A. Heinz

GIBBS·SMITH
PUBLISHER

SALT LAKE CITY

96 95 94 93 8 7 6 5 4 3 2 1

This is a Peregrine Smith Book, published by
Gibbs Smith, Publisher
P.O. Box 667
Layton, Utah 84041

Cover photograph: Chair from Ward W. Willits House and couch
    from William B. Greene House
Design by J. Scott Knudsen, Park City, Utah
Printed by Regent Publishing Services, Hong Kong

Library of Congress Cataloging-in-Publication Data
Heinz, Thomas A.
Wright, Frank Lloyd portfolio. Furniture / Thomas A. Heinz.
p. cm.
ISBN 0-87905-575-8
1. Wright, Frank Lloyd, 1867–1959—Themes, motives. 2. Architect-
designed furniture—United States—Themes, motives. I. Title.
NK2439.W75H45   1993
749.213—dc20   93-14074

INTRODUCTION

MUCH OF FRANK LLOYD WRIGHT'S furniture is quite comfortable. The strong geometry is often deceiving, since the points and angles are powerful. As Wright was constantly experimenting with designs, some are more successful than others. It may have been his intention for a chair back to hit right at the kidneys. More than anything else, the designs were to complement the spaces they were intended to occupy.

Wright designed more houses than any other type of building, thus most of his furniture is residential, for the dining room, living room, and bedroom. This gave him lots of chances to try many variations. There are nearly twenty different examples of a tall-back dining chair. Some have spindles; others have slats with and without pads or cushions. Much of the furniture that still remains in the buildings was built-in. Living-room seating and dining-room breakfronts make up the majority of examples.

Many Prairie-style houses have no known interior photos, no drawings, and nothing to indicate whether or not Wright created furniture for them. The Cheney House is an example; there are no known photos of the interior when it was occupied by the Cheneys and no furniture has come forward, so it is assumed that none was built. However, it is hard to imagine that Wright could not have convinced the Cheneys to commission furniture for such an important house.

In the not-too-distant past, Wright furnishings were bringing record prices at the auction galleries, so many houses were stripped of their original furniture and the pieces were sold at enormous prices. Also, because of this phenomenon, much furniture that had been removed from houses many years ago and probably not appreciated, surfaced. Most of the purchases were made by museums; as a result, original Frank Lloyd Wright furniture will be seen by a larger public. The down side is that the interiors no longer have the correct balance that they had with the furnishings in place.

As with buildings themselves, it is most important to see the designs in person. Most of the buildings open as house museums have new furniture designed for them. Some contain original pieces and others have contemporary reproductions.

There are two distinct periods in Wright's architecture, as well as his furniture. The Prairie period, mostly centered on his Chicago work, began about 1900 and ended in 1920. The Usonian period began with the design of three buildings: the Wiley House, Fallingwater, and Johnson Wax in the mid-1930s. The time in between is difficult to characterize, and very little work was built. The furniture of the Prairie period is mostly constructed in solid quarter-sawn oak. There was some use of veneer, but it was limited. It is difficult to determine the finish colors because of the chemical changes that have occurred over time, but mostly a medium to dark stain was applied to the oak and then it was varnished. In the Usonian period, the furniture was built from planes of plywood and was less sophisticated. Clients of lesser means were commissioning Wright, and the site carpenters were building the furniture and cabinets. All through his career, Wright was experimenting and a sense of excitement exists in all his work.

Thomas A. Heinz
The Gamble House
Pasadena, California, June 1992

FRANK LLOYD WRIGHT STUDIO, SPINDLE BOX CHAIR

Several of these cubic chairs were used in Wright's Studio reception hall and in the library. They are an elaboration of an earlier design for a cube chair. There are several variations of this chair in the Willits House and the Dana House. The Willits edition (on the front cover) has a taller back rail and the Dana edition has an insert to make it a reclining chair.

B. Harley Bradley House, Horizontal Slat Armchair

Awkward and gawky" are appropriate descriptions of this design, especially in view of the brackets that hold the arm and the unusual profile and angle of the legs. There is another similar example from the Bradley House, but with different side and back panels. Both of these are in sharp contrast to the simple and elegant designs that preceded the Bradley furniture.

WARD WILLITS HOUSE, SPINDLE ARMCHAIR

One of several pieces for the living room, all of which had spindle sides and backs. The odd thing about this design is that the spindles are vertical while the legs are angled. This causes some of the spindles to die into the front and rear legs. Was it that a different panel was to be installed in the place of the spindles or that they were remodeled later with the spindles added? This same remodeling occurred on Wright's own dining chairs and may have occurred here.

SUSAN LAWRENCE DANA HOUSE, DINING SET

This furniture represents the finest of all of Wright's designs for a dining room. The delicate tapers of the front legs and the rear rails, along with the single horizontal trim at the lowest edge of the seat, are features which present a balance and restraint that are in harmony with each other. The square-leg table is one of three that, when set together, seat forty guests. Wright's phrase about "taking great care with the ends, and the middle will take care of itself," is demonstrated in the line of the table spindles ending with a larger unit, and the entire length of smaller and larger spindles ending with the legs.

SUSAN LAWRENCE DANA HOUSE, MUSIC CABINET

For many years, the unusual nature of this fine piece of furniture led people to think it was a liquor cabinet. The small drawer at the top was thought to hold small glasses, while the art-glass section could hold decanters of brandy and other spirits. Apparently, it is actually a music cabinet. The bottom hinged door in the lowest section opens to a series of shelves that could hold music. What the art-glass section has to do with music is yet to be determined. In all, the piece is one of real curiosity. It is also one of the few designed to stand free and to include art glass.

DANA MEMORIAL LIBRARY, LOW-BACK CHAIR

As a memorial to her mother, Susan Lawrence Dana commissioned Frank Lloyd Wright to design a library for Lincoln School in Springfield. These chairs surrounded several tables in the library room. The room has been remodeled and the tables lost, but there are several chairs still in the Dana House. As noted in Henry-Russell Hitchcock's book *In the Nature of Materials*, there was a project completed for the Lawrence Memorial Library, Springfield, Illinois. Many thought it was a part of the Dana House. The volunteers at the Dana House discovered information of the existence of the library at nearby Lincoln School.

BOYNTON HOUSE, DINING ROOM

There are many Wright firsts in this room—for those who keep track of such things. The breakfront along the back wall was the first art-glass composition to include multiple panels. The dining table was the first to use light posts that have become so famous on the Robie House design. These posts make conversation quite awkward between adjacent diners at each end. They also interfere with arm movements of diners seated next to them. The chairs are unusual because the backs are not vertically plumb, as are nearly all other tall-back dining chairs designed by Wright.

LARKIN COMPANY ADMINISTRATION BUILDING, METAL DESK AND METAL SWIVEL ARMCHAIR

These are nearly the first metal office furniture produced. The desk chair was attached to either leg of the desk and could swing in and out of the knee hole. The back of the desk chair adjusts in pitch with a clever pin system and could be folded into the seat and pushed into the knee hole while the offices were cleaned each day. The perforated back of the armchair pivoted from an attachment at the center of the back. The writing surface of the desk was made from an early form of vinyl, called magnesite.

GEORGE BARTON HOUSE, DINING ROOM BREAKFRONT

*I*t is as hard to tell where the building ends and the furniture begins as it is to tell where the building ends and the garden begins. This breakfront can be considered a built-in piece of furniture. Its composition, consisting of a central drawer unit flanked on either side by tall cabinets, is typical of many similar units in other Wright-designed houses.

FOUR CHAIR DESIGNS

A rare assemblage of armless wood chairs from four well-known designers: Charles Rennie Mackintosh, Charles and Henry Greene, Frank Lloyd Wright, and Gustav Stickley. These chairs are on display in the front hall of the Gamble House in Pasadena. The strengths and weaknesses of these turn-of-the-century designs and designers can be compared and contrasted easily. The variations seen here show how nearly-the-same regard for materials and, in most cases, parallel theories of design, can have such divergent expressions.

ISABEL ROBERTS HOUSE, MIDDLE-BACK DINING CHAIR AND VERTICAL-SLAT RECLINING CHAIR

B oth of these chairs are from the house of the secretary to Frank Lloyd Wright. They were used in her Wright-designed house in River Forest and make one think that Isabel Roberts herself must have been a delicate, diminutive woman. The dining chair is quite light and not made of oak, as was most of Wright's furniture at that time. The beautiful book-matched wood grain on the panels of the recliner make this one of the most success-ful of all of Wright's reclining chairs.

ISABEL ROBERTS HOUSE, DINING TABLE AND DINING CHAIRS

The concept that all things relate to each other is legendary in the lore of Frank Lloyd Wright furnishings. It seems more correct to say that these things were in harmony rather than that they had any kind of mathematical or alignment relationships. This set certainly reinforces the harmonic theory. The tabletop is an unusual wood with very swirly grain. The chairs and the base, in contrast, are straight-grained.

AVERY COONLEY HOUSE, LIVING ROOM END TABLE

A fine design of Wright's, this end table is shown in a series of photographs of the living room of the Coonley House just after it was completed. In each photo, the table appears in a prominent location. Wright was known to have gone to these photo shoots, and it certainly looks as if he kept this table in view because he was so pleased with its design. There are actually two tables in one, with eight vertical members and three shelves. The sweeping legs give it a light, elegant flair.

ROBIE HOUSE, SLANT-BACK CHAIR

Many of Wright's buildings had slant-back chairs. The Larkin Building in Buffalo and Unity Temple in Oak Park are the most notable. The most unusual feature of Wright's slant-back chairs is that each one is a variation on the basic design. Some have square seats, while others have tapered ones. The blocks at the legs and tops of the rear stiles are omitted in several examples. The upper stretcher that guides the slanted backboard occurs at several different heights. Even the finger pull that is routed at the bottom of the upper rail is eliminated in one example, and a rectangular hole is punched right through the backboard. Apparently, the same drawing was not sent out to all of the furniture mills.

WILLIAM B. GREENE HOUSE, SPINDLE COUCH AND WARD W. WILLITS HOUSE, SPINDLE ARMCHAIR

There are few examples of free-standing multiple seating in Wright's work. Most of the couches and benches are built-in. There are chairs that have wood blocks at the top and/or bottom of the legs, but none have the big, flat feet that appear on the couch. The cantilevered seat recalls the many cantilevers in Wright-designed buildings. The Willits armchair is a development of the earlier example used in his Oak Park Studio (page 5). The sweep at the bottom of the legs makes it appear to be a solid, substantial design.

SHERMAN BOOTH HOUSE, CANOPIED BED

Wright's designs for beds are not well known and are rarely seen. They are as innovative as are any of his designs for other categories of furnishings. In his quest for new ideas, Wright tried many things. Not all of his experiments worked. While the canopy on this single bed gave a certain sense of comfort and protection, people also occasionally banged their heads on the projections.

SHERMAN BOOTH HOUSE, WALL SCONCE

There are very few wood wall sconces. The better-known examples are in the Francis Little House living room now at the Metropolitan Museum of Art in New York. The Booth example has a delicate cover with lots of very small sticks. There are many of these wall sconces throughout the house; they are in nearly every room. Wright's skill in proportioning designs is keenly demonstrated here.

SHERMAN BOOTH HOUSE, FLOOR LAMP

Most of Wright's lighting was built-in or attached to his buildings. There are only three designs for free-standing floor lighting. This design, the best of the three, is based on his Japanese-print frames designed for the exhibition at the Art Institute of Chicago in 1908. There are many parallel examples in Japanese design. These were designed at the time Wright was working on the Imperial Hotel for Tokyo.

F. C. Bogk House, Dining Room

Many unusual features are apparent in this dining set. The chair backs are angled from the seat up. The caned areas are only seen on some of the Imperial Hotel chairs and the prototypes of the Johnson Wax three-legged chair. The ebony insets in the table edge nearly reverse the precept of the nature of wood. Even the breakfront built-in with its integral lighting and Japanese art is unusual.

ALINE BARNSDALL HOUSE, HOLLYHOCK HOUSE, DINING SET

Wright takes a big left turn in the design of this unusual dining set. The back of this tall-back chair is supported by the spine in the center of the back rather than from the frame at the edge. The triangular table base replaces the legs at the corners. For such a grand house, the dining set seems small by proportion. There are cut-outs in the top of the chair back where ties to back cushions could be inserted.

Aline Barnsdall House, Hollyhock House, Tall-Back Chairs

Rarely do we get to witness a progression in design in a Wright building. Here we see a late development in the tall-back dining chair set to the right of a completely new idea in tall-back dining chairs. The similarities in the seats and proportions are carried over, but a strong decorative direction has arrived in the example on the left.

S. C. Johnson Wax Administration Building, Prototype Design for Secretarial Chair

This is at least the second actual prototype for the three-legged secretarial chair. The first had a caned seat and back with small-diameter pipe and webbed connections. It was painted white. This second model is of aluminum and constructed by a company owned by a client of Wright's from the 1890s, Warren McArthur. The U-support for the chair back was apparently too cumbersome and was simplified in the final design.

HERBERT F. JOHNSON HOUSE, WINGSPREAD, COCKTAIL TABLE

The development of plywood altered the aesthetic in Wright's later Usonian period. This table is one of a set that includes a hex end table and a hexagonal ottoman. All of these three designs have the same solid/void alteration scheme. The shelf under the top allowed for uncluttered storage.

HERBERT F. JOHNSON HOUSE, WINGSPREAD, LIBRARY DESK

These barrell chairs are a more modern simplification of those designed for the Darwin D. Martin House of Buffalo at the turn of the century. These chairs are not quite as solid as those are. The detailing of the dentils in the case-work is repeated in the free-standing end and cocktail tables. The lamp at the upper left is not a Wright design.

LLOYD LEWIS HOUSE, POLE LAMP

Many of Wright's Usonian houses (his later period) had examples of this wonderful lamp design. The Smith House in Bloomfield Hills, Michigan, and the Lovness House in Minnesota are two of the most noteworthy examples. The cedar reflectors make the quality of light quite soft and warm, providing a most pleasant overall light. There are many variations on these lamps where the boxes are 180 degrees from each other, and there are many examples of three- and five-light boxes. While appearing to be rather simple, upon further study, this design is quite complex.

Lloyd Lewis House, Side Chair

S imple but not very elegant, the use of plywood in this case is one of the most efficient uses possible of the material. Several can be set in a row and made into a bench, as in the Pope/Leighy House near Washington, D.C. These chairs were frequently cut and assembled on site by the carpenter-contractor. This made the houses inexpensive to furnish and guaranteed that there would be no incompatible designs introduced.

George D. Sturges House, Side Chair

Not every Wright furniture experiment resulted in a beautiful design. Although this chair is quite stable, it looks like it would tip over. Several of the houses designed during this period had designs like this one. The little key detail on the face of the front leg seems unnecessary.

HERMAN T. MOSSBERG HOUSE, HASSOCK AND END TABLE

Simply and elegantly proportioned, the hassock is made of cedar, as is the rest of the woodwork of the house. The end tables can be grouped and also will slip into the joints of the built-in cushion seating. The overall impression is one of elegant restraint.

HERMAN T. MOSSBERG HOUSE, PANELED ARMCHAIR

Slouching is not allowed in this chair, not because the back of the chair is not properly erect, but because there is not that much seat available. The panels serve as structural members and keep the thin frame square.

ROBERT LLEWELLYN WRIGHT HOUSE, COCKTAIL TABLE

The plan of this house is modeled after the American elm leaf, and this low table follows the design concept. The plywood legs are positioned like the veins of the leaf. The bottom shelf can hold a considerable quantity of books and magazines, allowing the top to be kept free of clutter so its form can be appreciated.

❦ Aline Barnsdall House,
   Hollyhock House, 1920
4800 Hollywood Boulevard
Los Angeles, California
pages 42, 44

George Barton House, 1903
118 Summit Avenue
Buffalo, New York
page 20

F. C. Bogk House, 1916
2420 North Terrace Avenue
Milwaukee, Wisconsin
page 40

Sherman M. Booth House, 1915
265 Sylvan Lane
Glencoe, Illinois
pages 34, 36, 38

E. E. Boynton House, 1908
16 East Boulevard
Rochester, New York
page 16

B. Harley Bradley House, 1900
701 South Harrison Avenue
Kankakee, Illinois
page 6

Avery Coonley House, 1908
300 Scottswood Road
Riverside, Illinois
page 28
Photographed at Kelmscott
   Gallery, Chicago

❦ Susan Lawrence Dana House,
   1903
Lawrence Avenue at 4th Street
Springfield, Illinois
pages 10, 12

Dana Memorial Library
   (demolished), 1905
Lincoln School
Springfield, Illinois
page 14

William B. Greene House, 1912
1300 Garfield Avenue
Aurora, Illinois
page 32 and cover
Photographed at Fifty/50 Gallery,
   New York

Herbert F. Johnson House,
   Wingspread, 1937
Four Mile Road
Racine, Wisconsin
pages 48, 50

❦ S. C. Johnson Wax
   Administration Building, 1936
1525 Howe Street
Racine, Wisconsin
page 46

❦ Larkin Company
   Administration Building
   (demolished), 1904
680 Seneca Street
Buffalo, New York
page 18
Photographed at Kelmscott
   Gallery, Chicago,

Lloyd Lewis House, 1940
Little St. Mary's Road
Libertyville, Illinois
pages 52, 54

Herman T. Mossberg House,
   1948
1404 Ridgedale Road
South Bend, Indiana
pages 58, 60

Isabel Roberts House, 1908
602 Edgewood Place
River Forest, Illinois
pages 24, 26

❦ Frederick C. Robie House,
   1909
5757 South Woodlawn Avenue
Chicago, Illinois
page 30

George D. Sturges House, 1939
449 Skyeway Road
Brentwood Heights, California
page 56

Ward W. Willits House, 1902
715 South Sheridan Road
Highland Park, Illinois
pages 8, 32, and cover
Photographed at Fifty/50 Gallery,
   New York

❦ Frank Lloyd Wright Studio,
   1897
951 Chicago Avenue
Oak Park, Illinois
page 4

Robert Llewellyn Wright House,
   1953
7927 Deepwell Drive
Bethesda, Maryland
page 62

❦ These properties are open for public tours.